Methuen Playscripts

The Methuen Playscripts series exists to
extend the range of plays in print by
publishing work which is not yet widely
known but which has already earned a
place in the repertoire of the modern
theatre.

TESTS

This is a selection from a series of some
fifty abstract and surrealist playlets
written between 1961 and 1964 in an
attempt to find valid ways of escaping
from a strictly realistic theatre. The
feel of these short sketches ranges from
hilarious verbal fireworks to fierce
frenzy and an unexpected lyricism.
Performance by a wide range of experi-
mental groups has left no doubt about
their dramatic effectiveness. Since the
first publication of this selection of
Tests in 1966 their interest and value
as texts for reading as well as workshop
use has also been established.

A METHUEN PLAYSCRIPT

Tests

PAUL ABLEMAN

First published 1966
by Methuen & Co Ltd
11 New Fetter Lane, London EC4
Reprinted 1969
Reprinted by Eyre Methuen 1972, 1974 and 1978
Printed in Great Britain by
Redwood Burn Limited
Trowbridge & Esher
ISBN O 413 31570 3

11 has previously appeared in <u>The Times Literar</u> <u>Supplement</u> 14 in <u>Underdog.</u>

There have also been performances at the Ben Uri Art Gallery, The Institute of Contemporary Arts, The Establishment, The Poor Millionaire, and by New Departures.

TESTS

1. TEST ONE
2. JOHNSON
3. ROSE
4. HELP
5. SHE'S DEAD
6. I EAT
7. NOW THAT I AM AN OLD MAN
8. ALIENS
9. ANOTHER LOVELY DAY
10. SPINE
11. WHAT IS THE PENALTY FOR NOSTALGIA?
12. AH SIMEON CREEL
13. EMILY AND HEATHCLIFFE
14. I USED TO HAVE A FRIEND

The first public performance of any of these TESTS was in a revue called 'Misshapes' at the Chanticleer Theatre London in 1962 produced by Tony Tanner in which numbers 2 and 4 were performed.

The TESTS included in this volume have subsequently been performed as follows:

'Help' (revue)
   National Drama League Theatre 1962   (2,3,4,9,10,12)
   Directed by Tony Carrick and George Little

'Theatre of Cruelty' season
   Lamda Theatre   January 1963   (5,6,10,13)
   Directed by Peter Brook

'One Hand Clapping' (revue)
   Lyceum Theatre, Edinburgh August 1964   (2,3,4)
   Directed by Charles Marowitz

B.B.C. Third Programme   1964   (2,4)
   Directed by Richard Thomas

Traverse Theatre Club and New Arts Theatre Club
   London   September - October 1965 (1,5,7,10,14)
   Directed by George Mully

Belgrade Theatre, Coventry   November 1965   (3,5)

TEST ONE

A: What would you do if you saw a man rolling like a wheel down a hill?

B: Hope.

A: No hope.

B: Kittens have spines. Anvils are delicate. Bill loves Sue.

A: Hope.

B: Hope.

A: No hope.

B: Hope.

A: A carpenter talked with a senator. A beekeeper preserved order. Oh, pharynx, where is thy sting?

B: Hope.

A: No hope.

B: No hope.

A: Hope.

B: Fleeing presumptive fleas. Willowy water-lust and traders. Here! Listen! Good thing! Bucks low.

A: No hope.

B: No hope.

A: No hope.

B: No hope.

A: A mammal of an estuary saluted a kindly laundryman. With a yelp the match teetered. Pickle all laundrymen. Toast archipelagos as if to pronounce renounce.

B: Yawn.

A: Hope.

B: Yawn.

A: Hope.

B: Yawn.

A: Hope.

B: Yawn.

A: Hope.

B: Yawn.

A: Hope.

B: Yawn.

A: Hope.

B: Yawn.

A: Hope.

B: Yawn.

A: Hope.

B: Can you spare a cigarette?

A: Hope.

B: Yawn.

A: Hope.

B: Yawn.

A: Hope.

B: Can you spare a tile for the roof?

A: No.

B: Can you cash a cheque? Especially if I decorate it with drawings of a fish?

A: No.

B: Last night in Minehead.

A: Last night in Yellowstone horrible park.

B: Last night in Minehead.

A: Last night and best night. What a fright. All my might.

B: Hope.

A: Hope.

B: No hope.

A: Hope no.

B: Hope no.

A: Hope no.

B: Hope no.

A: Hope no.

B: Hope no.

A: Hope no.

B: No hope.

A: Hope no.

B: Dear Robin, my sweet guide, nice codger, bellicose Roman, instructor, humble tyrant, belched.

A: Dear Robin. Dear Cock.

B: Robin's spirit yet stirreth. It starteth. Robin was a Minehead man.

A: What fortune! Dear Robin. Dear Cock. What hope?

B: Dear Robin never wore silk. He never groaned. He never piddled. He always piddled. He never groaned. He always piddled. He always wore silk.

A: Assuredly, this being towers.

B: No.

A: Hope.

B: No.

A: Hope.

B: No.

A: No.

B: No.

A: No. No. No. No. No. No. No. No.

B: Pigs should have passports. Hellish age is amongst us. One in every seven Canadian woodchucks despises leisure. The coat is rough-hewn. The coat is in the moat.

A: Bran, every time, for breakfast. Cook it valiantly. Eat with tongs. Now let's debate navigation.

B: Yes, assiduously.

A: Yes, assiduously.

B: Yes, assiduously.

A: What? Assiduously?

B: Not assiduously?

A: No not assiduously.

B: Why not assiduously?

A: Because of the ultimate destiny of all created things.

B: I'm a real delight.

A: So am I.

B: You're the bestest, dearest, wonderfullest, nicest, immaculatest, newest and everything. I like your tick.

A: Flick.

B: Tick.

A: Prick.

B: Nick.

A: Prick.

B: Sick.

A: You're a lovely bubble.

B: You're a pommy-peach. You're a munch-punch.

A: Pretty as pink.

B: You're a blithe bulge.

A: You're a lovely bubble.

B: Oh, Nan, be mine!

A: If Phelps permits.

B: You're semi-sweet.

A: Oaks should have passports.

B: Bliss.

A: Turnip.

B: Bliss.

A: Indeed, bliss to infuse all corporeal things with bliss.

B: Bliss indeed.

A: Indeed, bliss to litigate.

B: Indeed bliss.

A: Indeed bliss to piss.

B: Indeed bliss.

A: There's no certainly anywhere.

B: Cruel shapes—

A: Cruel shapes infest—

B: Cruel shapes infest-

A: Cruel shapes, harsh shapes-

B: Harsh shapes-

A: Infest-

B: Practising dieticians.

A: Cruel shapes infest-

B: Practising dieticians.

A: Harsh shapes infest-

B: Practising dieticians.

A: Cruel shapes infest-

B: Practising dieticians.

A: Cruel shapes-

B: Infest-

A: Practising dieticians.

B: Dismembered jackals strew the red streets. Oh jugular!
   Flaws protrude like enemies. Oh jaguar! Fanny, Fanny,
   come!

A: Hope.

B: Hope.

A: Hope.

B: Hope.

A: Hope.

B: Hope.

A: Hope.

B: Hope.

A: Hope.

B: Hope.

JOHNSON

1: Johnson.

2: Here.

1: Johnson.

3: Here.

1: Johnson.

4: Here.

1: All present and accounted for, sir.

5: Excellent. Now men, a word or two before you go. I have done the state some service, and they know it. No more of that. Are there any questions?

3: I have one or two questions, sir. I hope you won't be offended, sir. I mean, they may seem rather foolish questions, sir. Well, you're a great captain. I can see that at a glance. Your belt keeps bursting its buckles in the attempt to restrain your mighty gallant heart within.

5: Precisely.

3: And I'm only a poor squaddy called Jones.

5: Johnson, surely.

3: If you prefer, sir. Anything to oblige a mighty buckling general such as you plainly are.

1: Speak up, man.

3: These questions - well, frankly, sir, I was a bit worried about the danger.

5: What danger?

3: That's just the point, sir, what danger? Is there likely to be any danger?

5: I suppose so. There might be. You can never tell. Let's hope there isn't, what? Any more questions?

2: I've got a question, sir.

1: Speak up.

2: I'm going to speak up. Don't keep interrupting. I won't come at all if you don't stop bullying.

1: Speak up, Johnson.

2: My name isn't Johnson. Why do you call everyone Johnson?

5: Has there been a mistake on the nominal roll? Adjutant, er sergeant - what is your rank? I never learned the little badges properly.

1: My rank, sir?

5: Your rank, yes, your rank. Your er status in this er group er detachment - military assembly. What do they call you? How are you addressed?

1: How am I addressed, sir?

5: Well yes, I mean, are you a corporal?

1: No, I'm not a corporal.

5: Well are you er a colonel?

1: I don't think so.

5: Well be a bit helpful. What shall I call you?

1: Call me Johnson, sir.

5: All right, but it's not a rank. Everyone else is called Johnson too.

2: I'm not, sir. And that's my first question. If I'm to set off with you and these lads on an enterprise with any taint or whiff of danger about it, I want to know first of all why I have to be called Johnson?

5: I really don't know. Why do we call them all Johnson, er Johnson?

1: I don't know, sir. Isn't that their names?

5: Isn't that your names?

2: It's not mine.

3: My name's really Jones but I don't care.

4: I don't mind being called Johnson.

2: I prefer when embarking on some beastly adventure like this to be called by my real name.

5: Very well. What's your real name.

2: Johnson.

5: Call this man Johnson, henceforth, Johnson.

1: Very well, Johnson.

5: Sir, to you.

1: Very well, Sir Johnson.

5: Any further questions?

2: Yes, that was only my first. I don't like this set-up and I've got a good many questions I want to ask, sir.

5: Very well, but you know what they say: tomorrow and tomorrow and tomorrow is creeping in at a petty pace. So kindly get on with it, Johnson, before closing time. You'll all want a pint, I take it?

3: Your very good health, sir.

4: He's a grand indulgent admiral.

5: You see, the men are gasping. Get on with your questions.

1: Speak up! Speak up!

2: Where are we going?

5: I'm afraid that's a secret. Even I don't know that.

2: How are we going to get there, if you don't know?

5: Follow the others, I suppose.

2: What others?

5: The main force, damn it!

2: Well where is the main force?

5: I don't know where the blasted main force is. It's assembling somewhere, I suppose. Tell him where the main force is, Johnson.

1: I've no idea, Sir Johnson.

5: Well what good are you?

1: I'm a lot of good. I can sing and play the trumpet. I'm good at raping captive women, too.

3: Please, sir, I've thought it over and I'd rather be called Jones. You see it's my family name.

5: Very well. Any more questions?

2: Where are we going?

5: I don't know.

2: Well, you ought to know.

5: The hell with you.

2: I'm not coming.

5: Yes you are.

2: No, I'm not.

5: I'll put you in irons if you don't shut up. Put him in irons, Johnson.

1: We haven't got any irons, Sir Johnson.

5: No irons? Well bind him securely. I'm a mighty captain, but I get cheesed off with the troops, sometimes.

2: All right, I'll come. I've got some more questions but you've made me forget them, being so surly: I'll remember them soon, though.

3: You don't mind calling me Jones, do you, sir? It's the only thing I ask and after that I'll follow such a warlike figure as you are anywhere - up and down the thick and the thin, through terrible scuffles and gory conflict - all that I'll do just for the small, pious favour of using the old family name. I don't like being out of step with all you Johnsons but if you can accommodate one single Jones, sir, why you've got a loyal scuffler behind you who'll follow you in and out of brawling squabbles, loyal to the end, be it bitter or sweet, just for the simple favour of using -

1: Order! Order! Clear the court! Gag that joker!

5: Hold him Johnson! That's it! Clamp your hand over his mouth. The man's got the rhetorical horrors. If he goes on like that, he'll give our position away to the enemy. I'm not sure that he's any asset to the battalion. Now then, men, you've had a practical demonstration of the swift and vigilant discipline I maintain in my platoon. Is there a man in this division with mutiny in him? I thought so! A flash of the eye and the dogs quail. Now then, you quailing dogs, any final questions before closing time?

4: Can I bring my girl along, sir?

5: Your girl? I shouldn't think so, no. It doesn't sound regimental to me. What do you want your girl for anyway, man?

4: I like sleeping with her, sir.

5: What? I mean - damn it - sleep's sleep. Knits up the bedraggled sleeve of care and all that. Surely you can sleep with one of the Johnsons, can't you?

4: It's not the same, sir.

5: Well, what's the difference, in the name of Macedonian Philip?

4: She's built different, sir.

5: Is she? How?

4: Well she's got different parts.

5: What's that got to do with sleep?

4: Well I don't really want to sleep with her.

5: You just said you did.

4: I want to stay awake with her, sir. You get me, don't you?

5: Can't have that! You'll need your sleep. We're embarking on a gruelling adventure in a cruel testing ground and no man under my command is going to disgrace his lion-hearted commander for lack of sodding sleep.

4: I won't be awake all the time, you stupid idiot!

5: I'm not a stupid idiot.

4: You are too.

5: If you say that, I'll clamp you in irons.

1: We haven't got any irons, sir.

5: Well, he still mustn't say it. Tell him not to.

1: Don't call our gallant leader a stupid idiot.

4: He's being wilfully naive. Listen, sir, I only stay awake while we're doing it. After that, I get bags of sleep. It's lovely!

5: Really? And you couldn't do it with one of the Johnsons?

4: No, not for preference. It's not as nice, I don't think

5: All right, bring her along.

1: I think it's against regulations, Sir Johnson.

5: Is it?

1: I've got an idea it is.

5: Well you should have told me earlier. We've wasted a hell of a lot of good drinking time on this footling point. You can't bring your girl, Johnson.

4: Then I shall have a grudge.

5: Then you'll have to have a jolly old grudge.

4: In my opinion you lack the wisdom of the true commander.

5: Well, you still can't bring your girl. Now then, men, a little speech to inspirit you before the ordeal, whatever may befall, on the honourable field when we come to grips with the dread foe.

2: That was the other question. Who is the dread foe?

5: The French.

1: Sir Johnson, the French are our allies.

5: Exactly! The French and us are off to crush the er the Germans.

3: I thought the Germans were on our side now?

5: Astute man! I won't have my detachment ignorant of basic military realities. Glad you avoided that trap, Johnson. Now then, men -

2: Who are our foes?

5: Shut up!

2: I want to know the enemy.

5: The Saracens.

4: That was hundreds of years ago.

5: They're stirring again. But of course they're not the main enemy. The main enemy are the Scots.

1: No, Sir Johnson!

5: That is, the Irish.

3: I'm Irish.

5: The Carthaginians - the rebel colonies - the Zulus - the Europeans - the Orientals - the inhabitants of all continental land masses - the human race - the animal kingdom - living cells - biology - matter - energy - the cosmos -

1: Dismissed!

ROSE

1: Rose.

2: Rose.

1: Rose.

2: Rose.

1: Rose.

2: Rose.

1: Rose.

2: Bison.

1: Rose.

2: Bison.

1: Rose.

2: Rose.

1: Rose.

2: Rose.

1: Rose.

3: Bison.

2: Rose.

1: Rose.

3: Bison.

1: Rose.

2: Rose.

3: Rose.

4: Rose.

2: Bison.

3: Bison.

4: Bison.

1: Rose.

4: Dysmenorrhea.

1: Rose.

3: Rose.

2: Rose.

4: Rose.

2: Rose.

1: Rose.

3: Pigs.

1: Pigs.

2: Pigs.

4: Pigs.

2: Accommodation for single gentlemen.

4: Unprecedented pigs.

1: Accommodation for single pigs.

4: Unprecedented pigs.

3: Eggs.

1: Pigs.

2: Eggs.

4: Statesmen.

2: Eggs.

4: Statesmen.

1: Pigs.

4: Statesmen.

3: Eggs.

1: Abundant regenerative powers.

2: Thank God my wife and children are out of harm's way.

1: Abundant regenerative powers.

4: Accommodation for unprecedented pigs.

2: Thank God my pigs are out of harm's way.

3: Abundant regenerative wives.

2: Thank God my pigs are unprecedented.

1: Abundant accommodation for wives.

2: Thank pig I've never harmed any Gods.

4: Abundant accommodation for statesmen.

2: Thank God my children are pigs.

1: Eggs.

4: Pigs.

3: Rose.

4: Pigs.

2: Statesmen.

3: Rose.

1: Bison.

3: Rose.

2: Statesmen.

3: Rose.

1: Eggs.

2: Bison.

4: Tell me, monsieur, were you favourably impressed by our bison?

3: Yes.

4: You insist, monsieur, that your pigs suffer from dysmenorrhea?

3: Bien sûr.

1: Eggs are scarce this season because the chickens have all got dysmenorrhea.

3: Oui, je comprends.

2: Our policy is to separate the sheep from the bison.

3: Très bien. Bravo. And vot of your, how you say, statesmen?

2: Vot of them?

1: Vot of them?

2: Vot of them?

4: Vot of them?

3: Bien sûr. Très bien. Vot of them? Oui, je comprends.

4: Vot of them?

3: Très bien.

2: Vot of them?

3: Très bien.

1: Vot of them?

3: Alors, je dois partir. Au revoir, mes roses.

2: Au revoir.

1:   Au revoir.

4:   Au revoir.

2:   Au revoir.

1:   Au revoir.

4:   Au revoir.

2:   Bison.

HELP

1:   Help.

2:   The tulips are early this year.

1:   Help.

2:   How peaceful it is here, amidst this rural calm. Over there is a brawling stream. Just behind that brawling stream is a strange and unpleasant object.

1:   Help.

2:   My mind is a sea of calm, in spite of that unpleasant object, whatever it may be. But I am civilized and erenely self-possessed. Since there are no paintings or works of sculpture here, I shall read a book.

1:   Help.

2:   I don't seem to have a book on me.

3:   How peaceful it is here, amidst this rural calm.

2:   How delightful to hear my very thoughts expressed by another party.

1:   Help.

3:   Were those your very thoughts?

2:   Yes.

3:   Over there is a brawling stream.

2:   Exactly.

3:   And behind it there is something nasty.

2:   Let us purge the irritant from our consciousness.

3:   All right.

1:   Help.

3:   Do you come here often?

2:   Quite a lot.

3:   So do I. My name's Elizabeth.

2:   So is mine. My full name is John Elizabeth Butch Adele Plonk.

3:   My full name is William Elizabeth Helen Butch Reilly.

1:   Help.

2:   What do you do?

3:   I make contraceptive pills. What do you do?

2:   I trap stoats. But that's only a hobby. Normally I waste paper. Life is so full. Don't you ever feel that?

3:   I feel that very often. I feel it now, here in this charming spot. What's that nasty thing over there?

2:   I think it's Plato.

1:   Help. Help.

3:   Why doesn't he go away?

2:   Because he's a beast. But we won't let him spoil things for us, will we?

3:   I love you.

2:   I love you.

3:   I love you too.

2:   And I too love you.

3:   I loved you the very first instant I set eyes on you.

2:   It must have come over you like a road accident.

3:   It did. It zoomed down like a jet plane.

2:   It must have swept you up like a rocket.

3:   It made me whirl like a satellite.

2:   Love explodes within us like hydrogen heated to the critical temperature for one ten-millionth of a second by a conventional fission bomb.

3:   It's more insidious than neutrons.

2:   I don't think that can be Plato after all.

3:   Why not?

2:   It's not human.

1:   Help. Help. Help.

3: Elizabeth –

2: Call me John Elizabeth Butch Adele.

3: I have a confession to make.

2: What is it?

3: I'm not human either.

1: Help.

2: Aren't you?

1: Help. Help.

3: No. I'm a computer.

2: So am I.

1: Help.

3: Then our love has a secure foundation.

2: Have you noticed how early the tulips are this year?

1: Help. Help. Help. Help.

SHE'S DEAD

1: By jove, you've murdered that woman!

2: It's dreadful!

1: Why did you do it?

2: She provoked me. This is terrible.

1: You've killed her. You've taken a human life!

2: It's appalling! This is the most frightful thing that ever happened to me.

1: What have you done, man?

2: I think I've killed this woman.

1: Jove, how ghastly!

2: This is horrible. Yesterday – a year ago – how could I have dreamt ...

1: Look here, what have you done?

2: My God, she's dead!

1: How awful!

2: This is terrible.

1: Well, there's one fortunate thing.

2: Is there some consolation?

1: There's one very happy aspect.

2: Do you detect some glint of hope?

1: I'm a policeman. I can arrest you and make sure you pay the full penalty for your crime.

2: I say, that is lucky.

1: Strange that I should happen past, just after you'd done this dreadful thing.

2: It's almost miraculous, isn't it? Things are never quite as bad as they seem at first glance.

1: I'll see that you suffer.

2: I feel I can depend on you.

1: You'll sweat torments in a reeking prison, I'll ensure that.

2: It's very good of you.

1: By jove, what's happened here?

2: I've killed this woman.

1: What have you done?

2: I've taken a human life. I've broken the sternest law of God and man.

1: Thank God, I'm a policeman.

2: Thank God for that!

1: Anguish is your portion from now on, until we take your life in some disgusting way.

2: How will you do it?

1: We'll probably strangle you with a length of rope. Nightmares are mere diversion compared to what's waiting for you.

2: It's lucky you passed by.

1: My God, man, what have you done?

2: Constable, I - I've murdered this woman.

1: Why did you do it?

2: She picked a flower.

1: Provocation is no excuse.

2: She was my mother.

1: You've killed your mother. Matricide, you'll squirm! Your brain will buzz with horror until you crave the noose as a benefaction.

2: I loved this girl. She was a typist.

1: You've destroyed a typist, a useful citizen. Think of the letters that will blossom no more beneath her nimble fingers.

2: This woman was a barmaid.

1: The handle of the beer-pump will ne'er more feel her touch.

2: What have I done?

1: You've taken a human life. Now, the facts: How did you kill her?

2: With my penknife! Officer, officer, it was unpremeditated. I merely took out my knife to admire the silver blade and then I felt I should try it out. So I stabbed Lilly twenty-four times.

1: Look at her blood, her innocent blood!

2: I stabbed her twenty-four times.

1: See, her blood's come out. That'll teach you to play with penknives.

2: Her blood - I didn't think it would all come out.

1: She was a blithe girl, a healthy thing - tell me what she was?

2: A song!

1: Yes, she was a song, a healthy thing. What was this girl?

2: Light.

1: Of course, she was light - she was the air, the breeze, the ripple in the air, but there was blood inside her.

2: I pierced her veins.

1: What have you done?

2: Officer, I have a confession to make.

1: Oh yes, sir?

2: Yes, you see I seem to have - inadvertently of course - slain this girl.

1: I see, sir. You realize, sir, that I shall have to report this?

2: Is that absolutely necessary, officer?

1: It's the regulations, sir. I know that we often seem unnecessarily meticulous to the public but we have to register all misdemeanours.

2: I say, I hope this doesn't mean I shall have to appear in court?

1: Oh no, sir, I shouldn't think anything like that. We get dozens of these little incidents.

2: She was called Lilly, I think. You may want that for your records.

1: Why did you kill her, sir? I might as well take all the facts.

2: Why? Oh, I don't know. How can one assess every fleeting impulse? I met her in a pub, brought her out here to this remote spot, assaulted her -

1: Carnally?

2: Yes, you know, rape and then I thought I might as well kill her as anything else.

1: Right you are, sir, I've got that. Perhaps you'd give me your name and address, sir? Just for our files?

2: Is that really necessary?

1: Well I would be grateful, sir. My sergeant's a stickler for detail.

2: Very well, my name is Bill.

1: Bill, sir?

2: Bombay Bill, also known as The Slaughterer.

1: And your address, sir?

2: Skull Lane.

1: I say, what have you done?

2: Has something been done?

1: There's a dead girl here.

2: Did I do that?

1: Have you killed this human being?

2: Have I deprived someone of life?

1: At your feet, man, a dead girl!

2: A girl you say? One wanting life?

1: Why did you do it?

2: You imply that there's some way of knowing why things are done?

1: There's a gun here.

2: I fancy it's a revolver.

1: Is this your gun?

2: I have seen that weapon before.

1: Was this the cause of death?

2: A bullet leapt from its mouth.

1: This finger, this index finger on your hand - did it squeeze the weapon's trigger?

2: Pressure, generated by the muscles of my body, authorized by the synapses of my singing nerves, moved that little lever. The gun spat metal, a gob of metal which parted her soft tissues. I think it was then she died.

1: Have you slain this woman?

2: I? I have slain no-one. It was the gunmaker.

1: You killed this girl!

2: It was not I. It was a Hebrew who made the law she broke.

1: Then I must arrest you.

2: And are you really authorized to put a stop to history?

1: Jove, what have you done?

2: What I was told to do by the roots groping in the earth.

1: You've killed this girl.

2: By the numb stones nesting on the plain.

1: You'll pay for this.

2:   By my accomplice the' rain and his wild pal the wind.

1:   To the cells!

2:   Yes, come, brother, to the cells but first - wipe the blood from your hands too.

I EAT

1:   I eat.

2:   Feet.

1:   I eat.

3:   Velocity.

1:   I eat.

2:   I eat.

3:   I eat.

1:   I eat.

3:   Velocity.

1:   I am.

2:   Am am.

1:   Am am.

1:   Am am.

2:   Jolly.

3:   Am am.

1:   Am am am I am.

2:   Am am.

1:   Am am am.

3:   Am.

1:   Am.

2:   Jolly.

3:   Am jolly am.

2:   Am.

3:   Am jolly.

1:   Am am jolly am.

3:   Am jolly am am.

2:   Am am am am.

1:   Indestructible beatitude.

3:   Am am.

1:   Am am am am am am am.

2:   Am am am am am.

3:   Axe axe.

2:   Axe ex ex ex am ex.

3:   Axe am axe axe am.

2:   Am ex ex am ex ex.

3:   Borneo.

2:   Borneo.

3:   Jupiter.

2:   Borneo.

1:   Say.

3:   Say.

2:   Battle.

3:   Say battle.

2:   Say struggle.

3:   Say struggle.

1:   Struggle, struggle, say.

2:   Say.

1:   Say.

3:   Indestructible beatitude.

1:   Ellipse good.

2:   Yes, very good ellipse.

1:   Good ellipse.

3:   Toothache splendid.

1:   Splendid. Admirable toothache.

2:   Jolly.   Jolly.

3:   What's in the ocean?

1:   What's in the ocean?

3: A jolly octopus.

2: Jolly. Jolly.

3: A jolly octopus.

2: Jolly. Jolly.

3: A jolly octopus.

1: There's no man swimming. There are no warships.

3: There's a jolly octopus.

2: Jolly. Jolly.

1: There are no pythons. There are no warships. In the ocean are no banknotes.

2: There's one man swimming.

1: I think not.

3: One man might swim in the ocean.

1: I think not.

3: One man might.

2: Might.

3: One might, one man might.

2: Might.

1: Might.

2: Might.

3: Stir the living.

2: Revive the dead.

3: Shake the earth.

1: Might.

3: One man might.

1: Might, might.

2: I see.

3: Might.

2: I see.

1: Might.

2: I see.

1: See.

2:   I see.

3:   Might.

1:   Might see.

3:   Indestructible beatitude.

NOW THAT I AM AN OLD MAN

1:   Now that I am an old man, I realize certain things.

2:   You are certainly getting old.

1:   On the other hand, I am not an old man, but a very young one.

2:   You are rather old.

1:   Yes, you are right. I must be old because that seems to be the general opinion.

3:   That is not my opinion. What do you mean by old?

2:   Yes, what do you wish to convey when you suggest that you are old?

1:   I don't know.

2:   You are in a state of not knowing? Perhaps you don't care? Perhaps you don't care enough?

3:   That is not my opinion. What does he mean by old?

1:   I will think of examples of things that are truly old and I will confront you with these examples.

2:   I am ready for your examples.

3:   I too am ready for your examples.

1:   Air is very old. Clothes are very old. Light is very old.

2:   You are certainly getting old. On the other hand, you can never get old because you must always be the same age.

3:   What is the colour of a distraction?

2:   You are certainly very old, but you are also very nice. I love you more every moment. What is the colour of a distraction?

1:   A distraction is green. Age is green too. And I am green, green as air, green as clothes and green as light.

3: What else is green?

2: The question has been posed as to the total number of green things.

1: Unhappily there are only fourteen green things and they are all as old as fruit.

2: Perhaps we should know if they are as ripe as fruit?

3: Unhappily, nothing is as ripe as fruit. Faith is nearly as ripe as plums, but sexual passion is much less ripe than mangos.

1: If I am truly old, must I not then be a clock?

3: Unhappily none of us can escape sharing most essential characteristics with clocks.

2: The chief difference is that we do not click when we are opened.

1: Nor do we groan when we are wound.

2: Unhappily, we do groan when we are wound. It is agreeable to think that we can dance as blithely as clocks.

1: If I were not so old I would join your revels and dance until I turned green.

3: It would be appropriate for you to be green since you are Henrik Ibsen, the playwright.

2: It would be even more appropriate for you to wear lascivious garters.

1: It is fine to be green and Ibsen.

2: Since you are green and Ibsen and decked in lascivious garters we should dance and then go to a horse race.

3: And eat melons.

2: And mutton.

1: And time.

2: Green time.

1: Round as melons.

3: Lusty as mutton.

4: Lusty as mutton.

2: Can one dispense with perfect understanding?

1: Only when you are as old as I am.

4: Lusty as mutton.

1: Old sailors, such as I, never forget the sea.

3: The sea is like a small violin.

4: It is lusty as mutton.

3: It is like a small violin, shaped like the fingernail of a deposed monarch.

4: It is like the bewilderment of a deposed monarch. It is thus lusty as mutton.

3: It is like the ecstatic despair of the subjects of a deposed monarch, as they pillage the monarch's kennel.

4: It is like that nasty grass that stings but tastes nice to sheep and pink snakes. All pink snakes are old, and glow at night.

3: And eat mutton.

2: Green mutton.

1: Older than me.

3: I suppose that formerly you had a picture of the world, but now you lack all but creature comforts?

1: That is exactly the case.

4: A small violin case. A hard case. A dangerous case. It is a case of swimming in the pink sea with pink snakes writhing all around.

1: Just then, for the first time, it happened: I forgot the sea.

3: In that case, you are no longer old, Ibsen.

2: Twenty things just happened to me.

4: Yes, I observed them. Seven were made of ivory, one of steel and the rest of boiled sugar. Ninety things just happened to me.

3: Tell us about one of them.

4: I would tell you about the best but it is intimately connected with the worst. The second best is attached to the fourteenth and seventeenth worst and interpenetrates with seventeen others. The third and fourth best are intrinsically trivial. Perhaps the thirty-seventh would please you most.

1: I know it already, it is the violin of the sea that I have forgotten.

4: That is correct.

3: Did it happen swiftly?

4: As History.

2: Did it happen joyously?

4: As carpets.

1: Is it suitable for a lad like me?

4: No, quite unsuitable.

1: It is nearly time for us to reproduce.

3: How many of us will there be then?

4: As many as there are flies in a cathedral.

2: More.

3: Really? What formula are you using?

2: The mighty Chutney calculus. It's the best way of reckoning anything.

4: Like how much despair is required to shatter consciousness.

1: Like how many gonads are required to fertilize time.

3: Using that method, would you tell me, what is the lowest level of awareness that will sustain gravity? No, let me rephrase that question, what is the greatest number of objects that can be made to disappear?

2: The answer is hazelnuts.

4: We have gathered here today to praise our great colleague Ibsen for his mighty achievement in painting "Madame Da Vinci prostrate on a grid". Of his lesser-known achievements, we need only mention his design for a phallic totem to be installed in the Burnley Branch of the Y.W.C.A. Congratulations, Henrik Ibsen of Nyasaland.

1: I am proud to be a Nyasa man. A stick of liquorice would be ample reward for my efforts.

3: We intended to present you with a naked little girl.

1: Couldn't I have the liquorice and the girl?

2: Yes, you can have both the liquorice and the girl and a pair of slippers made out of melons.

3: Green as melons.

2: Lusty as mutton.

4: That fit like time.

ALIENS

1: Plato.

2: Plato.

3: Baked beans.

2: Plato.

3: Plato was a celebrated Greek banana salesman.

2: Plato.

1: Plato.

2: Plato.

1: Plato.

2: Plato.

1: Plato.

2: Charles Dickens.

1: Plato.

2: Plato.

3: Charles Dickens was a celebrated Greek banana grower. He sold tons of bananas to Plato. Plato resold them to the Athenian public, making a profit of nearly two hundred per cent.

4: Plato came to my house and stole a leg of beef. After that we refused him all hospitality. He retaliated by setting up a micro-wave transmitter in the street and guiding bats into our living room.

2: Is that because he was really an alien from outer space?

4: That is our opinion. We firmly believe that Plato must have been a visitor from outer space. He may have been a spy.

2: He may have come with instructions to contact Old Uncle Tom Cobbley, who was also a spy from outer space. Our society is, and always has been, riddled with spies from outer space.

1: They probably want to steal our defence secrets. If you dissect a spy like Plato you find there are glittering electrons inside him. There are only two alternatives. Either they must be executed and this is far from easy since they glow with a tough, alien, star-nourished vitality which defies our normal methods of execution or they must be ejected, that is hurled beyond our gravity in rocket-tombs. The government, very creditably, has adopted the latter alternative and most alien spies have already been ejected.

4: Plato was a Greek philosopher. He wrote numerous Socratic dialogues and founded the idealist school of philosophy.

3: Charles Dickens.

4: Pickled herrings.

3: Charles Dickens.

4: Pickled walnuts.

3: Charles Dickens.

4: Roast pork.

3: Charles Dickens.

1: Pickled Dickens.

3: Charles Pickle.

1: Pickled pickle.

3: Dickens Dickens.

1: Pickled pickle.

3: Dickens.

1: Pickle.

3: Dickens.

2: Charles Dickens was a celebrated Greek fishmonger. He had a skin that was as white as snow.

3: I always heard that it was as white as typing paper.

1: I always heard that it wasn't white at all but blue, blue as the sea that chafes round Sunium.

4: Perhaps Charles Dickens was really a chameleon?

2: The chameleon is a genus of reptile with a long, prehensil tongue, independently swivelling eyes and a photosensitive epidermis capable of mimicking the hue of its immediate environment.

4: That sounds like Dickens alright.

1: It sounds to me more like Plato, the last king of Africa.

3: It makes me think of William Shakespeare, the German chemist.

1: It brings to my mind Michaelangelo, the victor of Hastings.

3: It carries my thoughts to Helen, the famous air hostess.

1: It evokes for me King Arthur, the furniture magnate.

3: It transfers my imagination to Dr Johnson, who wrote "The Sexual Life of the Poets".

2: Plato.

3: Who?

2: Plato.

4: Who?

2: Plato.

4: Plato?

2: Of course.

1: Plato?

2: Of course.

3: Plato?

2: Of course.

1: Plato?

2: Of course.

1: Plato?

2: Of course.

1: Plato?

2: Of course.

1: Moby Dick?

2: Of course.

1: Henry the Eighth?

2: Of course.

1: Oscar Churchill?

2:   Of course.

1:   Winston Wilde?

2:   Of course.

1:   Plato?

2:   Oh yes.

1:   Plato?

2:   Oh yes.

1:   Prester John?

2:   Oh yes.

1:   Mary, Queen of Turks?

2:   Oh yes.

1:   Alexander the Mote?

2:   Oh yes.

1:   Timothy Tuppence?

2:   Oh yes.

4:   Aliens? All? All from outer space?

3:   All. All wanderers, pilgrims, vagrants of the vacuum?

2:   Oh yes.

3:   What is thought?

2:   Dust in the living room.

3:   What is life?

2:   The frailty of matter.

3:   Who is Plato?

2:   You.

3:   An alien with electrons inside?

2:   Yes.

3:   Will I live forever?

2:   You already have.

ANOTHER LOVELY DAY

1:   Another lovely day.

2:   I've been reading that business leaders have the opinion that no one has enough enterprise. Do you agree?

3:   My plan is simple. I shall go to Scotland.

2:   We three - we're real friends!

1:   Now listen Richard ...

2:   Angus.

1:   Anyway, listen, I was talking with your mother ...

2:   When?

1:   Tuesday. Your mother is a sweet, dignified, sexy old tramp.

3:   What's it like in Scotland?

2:   Worse than anywhere else.

3:   Where should I go then?

1:   It's immaterial. You're dead anyway.

2:   My name isn't Angus after all. It's Kit.

3:   What's it like in Scotland?

2:   If you like terror spiced with loyalty, you'll like Scotland.

1:   You'll love Scotland if you're fond of anguish beaten into routine.

3:   What are the girls like in Scotland?

2:   Sickly.

3:   What's art like in Scotland.

2:   Tremendous.

1:   Business leaders are of the opinion that one colossal heave will be enough.

3:   What then?

1:   Another colossal heave.

3:   What then?

1:   Death.

3:   Your cousin Martha was under the road bridge with a damned physician yesterday, Kit.

2:   Thank you for remembering my name. Would it make sense to sit still forever?

1: It's debatable. For myself, music and after music, cheese.

3: For myself, birds. And after birds, your cousin Martha, Kit.

2: Thank you for remembering my name.

3: Your cousin Martha, Kit, has qualities. I like a girl that likes doctors.

1: Do you know the most that any man sees of a girl? One half. Most men see only one-hundredth of a thousand girls, a thousandth of a million girls and so on. You only see flashes of everyone.

2: Thank you for remembering my name.

3: What are the girls like in Scotland.

1: Like leaders of industry.

3: What's art like in Scotland?

1: Like a dragon.

2: A little while ago I thought we were friends. Now we hate each other.

3: It's built in!

2: Thank you for remembering my name.

1: How's science doing?

2: About the same.

3: I'm glad that we three are scientists.

1: Check the reading.

2: Check the reading.

3: Up she goes.

1: Now let's have a go at Mars.

2: Here, chief, something's wrong. I can't find Mars.

1: Where's Mars got to?

3: What's that over there? Is that Mars?

1: No, that's Scotland.

3: That'll do.

1: Check the reading.

2: Check the reading.

3: Up she goes.

2: Do you ever get a lingering sadness?

3: Yes.

2: What does it make you think of?

3: Rape.

1: The last leader of industry that I spoke to was a thin man from the Isle of Wight. I particularly remarked about him the quality of abysmal stupidity.

3: The last girl that I had relations with was your cousin Martha, Kit.

2: Name's Abelard, Peter Abelard. What sort of relations did you have with my alleged cousin Martha?

3: Sinister ones.

1: What's happened to Kit?

2: Do you mean Kit Abelard? He was here a minute ago.

1: Where's here?

2: Here is where the race is.

3: To the left of Orion. What happened to Kit Abelard?

1: They got him with a poisoned ideal. He spun round three times, crying: faggots, for the furnace of desire! and then disappeared over the border.

2: Thank you for remembering my cousin Martha. A name, a form, a ghost.

3: Things are either infinitely divisible or an ultimate unity, death or life.

3: How's the ice-cream in Scotland?

1: Tastes of atoms.

2: How's the pee in the sewer, the drake on the pond?

1: Toiling.

2: How's the bubble in the field-marshal's throat?

1: Bubbling.

3: How's the architecture?

1: Demented.

3: You're wrong there. It may be a botched job but it's the best we've got.

2: Would you say it was a priceless heritage?

3: All the way.

2: Can any one recall my name?

1: Joseph.

2: And what of the associations?

3: Join them and convert them to our way of thinking.

1: My way of thinking is a wave that behaves like a particle.

3: My way of thinking is curved through infinite conceptual dimensions.

2: Mine is the eternal and inescapable burden of mitosis.

1: Lisp to me of love.

2: Once a man heard a knock at the door and he went to that door and he opened that door.

1: Excellent.

2: Once a man heard a knock at the door and he went to that door and he opened that door.

3: Before he did that, before he opened that door, he turned certain things over in his mind. Unfavourably impressed by their appearance he turned them back again.

1: This was a man known as Colin Pollen.

2: Once a man heard a knock at the door and was deeply surprised because he lived in a mine where there were no doors.

3: Before the surprise he allowed a torrent of thoughts to flood through his mind. After that came the surprise.

1: He was the manager of the mine and the sole operative. It was his job to disembowel the world.

3: The mine was a billion miles deep.

2: Colin lived alone there with Ganghis Khan. They both worked hard in the mine.

1: Nevertheless they had curtains with pictures of anteaters on them.

3: The mine was a million miles deep. But it wasn't very wide.

2: And it had no doors.

1: As a matter of fact they weren't men at all, they were anteaters.

3: Nor did they live in a mine but in a small cottage by the seashore.

2: With numerous doors.

1: It was their invariable habit to address each other in crisp tones.

3: Like leaders of industry.

1: Like your cousin Martha, Abelard.

2: I am a great man and I have no balls.

1: What's the essential difference between oranges and the Holy Ghost?

3: The same as that between trespass and leather boots.

2: My cousin Martha is a mere pulse. She has less integrity than my cousin Martha.

3: Moreover she lives a submerged existence.

2: There's no solution that I can see. It's a horrid bother to us all.

1: Has she seen a good doctor?

2: Yes, she has seen many good doctors.

1: What is their verdict?

2: They think it's psychosomatic. But how can this be? A young maid blossoming like an anteater should be fit.

1: What is her basic trouble?

2: She has no arms or legs.

1: Beyond that?

2: She has no teeth, no nose, no eyes, no appendix, no appetite, no location, no liver, no direction, no texture, no composition, no brain, soul, heart, mind, ambition.

3: Then she must be a figment.

2: How dare you say that about my cousin Martha?

3: I dare say it because I have a degree.

1: I dare dream because I am independent.

2: Even if I were excused I would not dare to love.

3: We live inside a trick.

2: A clever trick.

3: A deadly trick.

1: There is no air outside the trick.

3: I cannot breathe inside the trick.

2: Some of us must suffocate.

3: Tell them at last: nothing is blue.

1: Hello? I say - Hello? Hello? Hello? Hello? Hello?
    Hello? Hello? Hello? Hello?

SPINE

1: Spine.

2: Spine.

3: Dogma.

2: Dog.

3: Spice.

4: I called once.

3: Spice.

4: I called.

2: Spice.

4: Having called, I then.

1: I retreated.

4: I then.

1: I advanced.

4: I then.

3: Was your car damaged?

2: Yes.

3: Was your car damaged?

2: No.

3: Was your car damaged?

2: Spice.

3: Was your car damaged?

2: Spice.

3: Was your car damaged?

2: Was. Was. Was.

3: Was your car damaged?

2: Was.

3: Was your car damaged?

2: I was. I was. I was. I was.

3: I was.

4: I was.

1: I was.

2: I was. I was.

1: I was.

3: Your was. Car was.

4: Car was. Car was.

3: Your was.

2: Car was.

1: I was.

4: Car was. Car was. Car was.

3: It was damaged.

4: Car was damaged.

2: Spine was damaged.

4: Dogma remained intact.

1: How was dog?

4: Dog remained intact. Dogma was damaged.

1: How was dogma?

4: Dogma remained intact. Dog was dog.

1: How was dog?

4: Dogma remained dog. How was dogma?

1: Dogma was dogma.

4: How was dog?

1: Dogma was dogma?

4: How was dogma?

1: Dogma was dogma.

4: Was dogma dogma?

1: Dogma. Dogma.

3: Dogma.

1: Dogma.

2: Dogma.

4: Spice.

2: Dogma.

3: Antelopes.

2: Dogma.

3: Nitrogen.

2: Dogma.

3: Castanets.

2: Nitrogen.

3: Castanets.

1: Dogma.

3: Castanets.

4: We are an island people.

3: We call spice.

2: We play.

3: Castanets.

2: Never do we play.

3: Castanets.

1: Because we are.

4: Antelopes. We play.

3: We are island.

4: Antelopes. And we play.

2: We are island castanets.

4: And we play.

3: Nitrogen. Never do we play.

4: Nitrogen. Never do we play.

1: Nitrogen. Because we are.

2: Spice. We are spice without.

1: Dogma. We are nitrogen without.

3: Spice. And we play.

4: Observe us at play.

3: Watch us play.

4: Kindly watch us play.

1: We play at nitrogen.

4: We play at spice.

1: We play at nitrogen.

3: We play at antelopes.

1: At nitrogen. We play at nitrogen.

2: And spice.

1: We play at nitrogen.

2: We play at spice.

3: Watch us play.

4: Watch us.

3: Watch us play.

4: We do not wobble as we play.

3: Watch us.

2: We do not quibble as we play.

3: Watch us.

4: We sometimes gabble as we play.

3: The games are over now.

1: Feet.

3: The games are over now.

2: Septicaemia.

3: There are no games.

2: Septicaemia.

3: There are no games.

4:   Grit.

3:   There are no games.

2:   Septicaemia.

3:   I had a dog.

1:   I had a dog.

3:   I had a dog.

2:   I had a dog.

3:   I had a dog.

4:   I had a dog.

3:   I had a dog.

1:   Dog.

WHAT IS THE PENALTY FOR NOSTALGIA?

1:   What is the penalty for nostalgia?

2:   Ten days in prison or a fine of fifty pounds or both.

3:   What is the reward for close scrutiny?

2:   A healthy mind in a porcelain jug. The reward for unremitting attention to detail is beatification.

4:   I was beatified last year, but not for unremitting attention to detail.

1:   What were you beatified for?

4:   For discovering a new hormone.

3:   What does the hormone do?

4:   It grows chins on idiots.

1:   What's it like being beatified?

4:   Fair.

2:   What is the penalty for conspiring to overthrow a piece of abstract sculpture?

3:   Hormone treatment. The penalty for hope is despair.

1:   What's despair like?

3:   Like speech. The penalty for speech is space.

4:   What is the reward for serious intentions?

2:   The same as that for industrious sobriety. The reward for heroism is a wad of old chewing gum.

1:   What is the penalty for plotting to enthrone reason?

3:   Space. The penalty for visionary foresight is also space.

2:   Is there any incentive for elevating the standard of living?

1:   Yes, the incentive for elevating the standard of living is a signed volume of Swedish grammar.

4:   Who signs the volume.

1:   Edgar Bottle.

2:   Who is Edgar Bottle?

1:   A stevedore who lives in Wapping. The incentive for striving to create heaven on earth is a pat on the back by a trained armadillo.

3:   Who trains the armadillo?

1:   Edgar Bottle. He also trains fossils to reveal the secrets of evolution.

4:   What is the reward for fostering evolution?

2:   Three rectal suppositories. The punishment for impeding evolution is also three rectal suppositories. In either case they are administered in brisk sequence by a nimble squirrel trained by Edgar Bottle.

4:   Who is Edgar Bottle?

2:   The Prime Minister of the moon. He used to be a bent lawyer in Carlisle, but he was unanimously elected by the seven extra-galactic spores which inhabit the moon to be their chief representative.

3:   What is the encouragement given to protecting the innocence of children?

1:   There is no official encouragement given to protecting the innocence of children. Unofficially a squashed rose is sometimes bestowed. These are obtained from the huge, squashed rose nurseries that have recently been established in neuter county by an innocent child called Fanny Pizzle.

2:   Is there any penalty for prolonged observation?

1: The penalty for prolonged observation is space.

4: Is there any reward for perpetual vigilance?

3: A kiss from Madeleine Fob.

1: Who is Madeleine Fob?

3: A hirsute spinster who lives in Peru. The punishment for genuine originality is life imprisonment.

1: What is the reward for penetrating the secrets of the universe?

2: Evolution. The punishment for evolution is space.

3: Who administers all rewards and punishments?

1: Edgar Bottle. Good night.

AH, SIMEON CREEL

1: Ah, Simeon Creel, what an extraordinary length of time it is since we last met.

2: Ah, Simeon Creel, what an extraordinary length of time it is since we last met.

3: We last met, as I recall, in Yffle, the capital of Grapp.

2: I believe you're right.

1: How are your servants? How is your dog, Sprog?

2: Ah, Simeon Creel, what an extraordinary length of time it is since we last met.

1: How is your dog, Sprog?

2: What's that?

1: How is your dog, Sprog?

2: It's a dog. I call it Sprog.

1: How is your dog, Simeon Creel?

2: It's a dog. It's called, Sprog, Simeon Creel. It's a dog. It's called ...

1: How are your servants?

2: What's that?

1: How are your servants?

2: Ah, Simeon Creel, what an extraordinary length of time it is since we last met.

1: How are your servants? Does the one still comfort you? The one called Prknga?

2: Ah, Simeon Creel, what ...

1: I asked - I say - your servants! Listen!

2: Oh yes! I was having a quiet chuckle. Chuckling inwardly. I'm afraid I missed your last remark.

1: Yes, I made a remark.

2: Your name, sir?

1: Ian, as you well know, Simeon Creel. You undoubtedly remember Ian.

2: Ian?

1: Ian Creel.

2: Creel?

1: No, not Creel.

2: Of course not Creel. I'm Creel.

1: Not Creel. Not Creel. Ian - Ian ...

2: What was your remark, Ian Creel?

1: Not Creel. Not Creel. Ian - Ian ...

2: Of course not Creel.

1: Of course not.

2: How are your servants? Does the one still comfort you? The one called Prknga?

1: The one called Prknga?

2: Ah, Simeon Creel, what an extraordinary length of time ...

1: No, no, no, no, no.

2: You were right, you know. You've always been right. Ian was always known in Yffle as a man who would be right. Ian would be right when no-one else was right. I remember it well. Many's the inward chuckle I've enjoyed at the discomfiture your rightness strewed everywhere. You strewed discomfiture everywhere, Ian.

1: In Yffle. Ah, in Yffle. No, I was hardly such a wraith, such a casualty, as you suggest. Not in Yffle. No, not in Yffle.

2: Discomfiture attended you. You had a nimbus, an aura, a field of pure discomfiture which never left you. My servant, Prknga, feared you. He retreated when you approached. He would shudder and say; "Master Ian - him come!" He would tremble beside me like my dog, Sprog. You would emerge from the Sporkwood plantations, ruddy in the torrid sunlight, lucent in the brilliance, glistening in your aura of discomfiture.

1: In Yffle - yes, in Yffle, surely I was often wrong! You must admit I made mistakes in Yffle.

2: Yes, you did! Ah, Simeon Creel, what an extraordinary ...

1: Simeon! Simeon!

2: With your dog, Sprog, in Yffle.

1: You're wandering. It's painful. I find it painful to see you wandering, Simeon Creel.

2: Lagoon. Lagoon. Delightful word.

1: Ian Lamprey-Tram.

2: Is that your name?

1: Yes. It's Ian Lamprey-Tram. I was in Yffle for many years. I went to Yffle in a boat.

2: Do you like the word: lagoon?

1: Office work, of course. I wasn't very good at it. But I had friends. The company was good.

3: Here's your tyre, sir.

1: What did we do in Yffle? We grew Sporkwood. We cultivated Sporkwood using the local Yimba tribe for labour. Oh I suppose we had fifty-thousand acres under cultivation. That's enough Sporkwood to line half the world's toilet seats. There's nothing like Sporkwood for toilet seats.

2: How can I believe that? I'm a credulous man. I had a servant called Prknga. He could deceive me. He did deceive me. I'm a gullible man.

1: Quantities of Sporkwood. You were a planter, man,

one of the greatest. Why do you deny it? You know how much Sporkwood we grew.

2: My servant, Prknga, was - no - well - I admit far more than a servant. My servant, Prknga, might announce dinner. No, let us say he would take alarm and say that a Brindoo had broken into the farm and eaten three of the Tuks. It might not be true. I might find the rascal was deliberately deceiving me so that he could get at the whisky.

1: You trust me, Simeon Creel. You trusted me with your life. I have never forgotten.

2: Can I believe you? Trust? Certainly, but can I believe you. You blunder so. In Yffle you had the reputation of being a blunderer. You cast a cloud, a shadow, a projection of error around you. Simple things became elaborate. Shining truth wilted in your presence and died like a twelve-year old bull Gukne, bellowing piteously.

1: Someone seems to have brought me a tyre.

2: Ah, Simeon Creel, what an extraordinary length of time - ah, Simeon Creel! Ah, Simeon Creel!

1: Rapturous! What a delightful, witty chap! I'd forgotten what a feast you were, Simeon Creel.

2: That chap's brought you a tyre.

3: That chap's brought you a tyre.

1: That chap's brought you a tyre.

2: Bellowing like a twelve-year-old bull Gukne.

3: It's a tyre, not a lagoon. I fear it's only a tyre, sir.

1: It's not a lagoon.

3: It's a lagoon, sir. It's a little lagoon. Is that what you wanted?

2: Ian! Ian!

1: Simeon!

2: Ian!

3: It's a little lagoon. It's not a tyre.

2: What? Ian? Where? Yffle? Where?

1: Yffle. The sporkwood plantations.

2: Last year?

3: It's a tyre. It's not a lagoon. Didn't you want a tyre?

1: Last year? Yes? No?

2: The year before?

1: The year before?

3: I've got a smashing girl.

2: Ian Sprog, you know. Sprog died.

1: Last year? I'm not sure.

2: Sprog died, you know. Sprog is still with me, of course. Ian, that chap's brought you a lagoon.

3: That chap's brought you a lagoon.

1: A red lagoon.

3: That chap's brought you a lagoon.

1: A red lagoon.

3: That chap's brought you a lagoon.

1: A lagoon.

3: I'm a pornocrat.

1: A lagoon.

3: I've brought you a lagoon. Did you order a lagoon?

1: Simeon Creel! Oh, Simeon, how good it is to see you once more!

3: Hello.

2: This is a good tyre.

3: Of course, you're Ian Prknga. I'd - I'd - frankly I couldn't remember ...

2: This tyre is without value.

1: We met in Traaa, the capital of Binagonia.

3: In Traaa. Across the sea. At the home of the bishop of Traaa.

1: I have devilish pains in my thorax.

2: I have pains in my thorax.

1: I have devilish pains in my thorax.

3: I haven't got any pains in my thorax.

1: I have definite pains in my thorax.

2: Eat fish.

1: I have decided pains in my thorax. I wake up sweating from the pains in my thorax. The best dreams are mockery and the others are pain. We can stand pain without dreams, or dreams without life.

3: How long is it since you left Traaa?

1: I left Traaa eleven years ago. You will remember, Simeon, that I was appointed manager of the largest Doolah Plantation in Traaa. What you may not have realized is that the world market for Doolah was in decline due to the unfortunate but inevitable development of synthetic constituents very nearly as tough and durable as Doolah itself. My job, therefore, to mutter the least of it, was a thankless one.

3: How long is it since you left Traaa?

1: I left Traaa just nine months ago. At that time the Doolah crop, in greater demand than ever before, due to the development of manufacturing processes in several new industries that were based indispensably upon the supple and delicate texture of Doolah, had failed due to a local insurrection of operatives. My task therefore was hardly an enviable one. My servant, Trog, and myself escaped by night in a helicopter and flew straight to Wanjaini land. There the governor received me in a palace of pink peppermint. My servant, Trog, and my dog - whose name eludes me - escaped by night in a speedboat. We crossed Lake Wanjaini and reached the frontier of ...

3: How long is it since you left Traaa?

1: It is a long time since I last saw Traaa. Nevertheless my memory will never relinquish that strange, bitter and yet mysteriously affecting land: the steady rush of the Orsoo over the waving Doolah with the Panpans chanting as they rhythmically harvest the succulent crop. I wouldn't go back, mark you. From what I read in the Times one wouldn't know the place any more. No, sir!

3: Are you going back to Traaa?

1: Ah, Simeon Creel, what an extraordinary length of time it is since we last met.

3: Ian! Ian Lamprey-Tram! Is it really you?

1: How is your dog? Your dog, Sprog?

3: How is my dog, Sprog?

1: How is your dog, Sprog?

3: How is my dog, Sprog?

1: And your servant, Wanjaini? Who used to comfort you?

3: My servant Wanjaini? You ask about my servant Wanjaini?

1: And your dog, Sprog.

3: Wind dropping. Glad of that.

1: Lagoon. Sensuous word lagoon.

3: Wind dropping. But, Simeon, dogs are not whales. Dogs are not elephants. They are not parrots.

1: How is your dog, Sprog?

3: Sprog died many years before I left Doolah and it is now many years since I left Doolah. Wanjaini! Wanjaini!

2: Sir?

3: You recall Mr. Creel? Mr. Simeon Creel?

2: Yes sir. I remember Mr. Creel.

1: Go on, Wanjaini, you can't remember me.

2: Yes sir. I remember.

3: You remember?

2: Yes sir. I remember.

1: You remember?

2: Yes sir. I remember.

1: You remember?

2: Yes sir. I remember.

1: You remember?

2: Yes sir. I remember.

1: You remember?

3: You remember?

4: You remember?

5: You remember?

2: Yes sir. I remember.

4: The buffalos?

2: Yes sir. I remember.

5: The waves, the lagoon, the waves?

2: Yes sir. I remember.

3: The skin, the sweat, the body, desire, desire, desire?

2: Yes sir. I remember.

5: What do you remember?

4: How do you remember?

2: Yes sir. I remember.

4: How?

5: How?

3: How?

1: How?

2: I remember. Yes. I remember. I remember. Yes. I remember. I remember. Yes. I remember.

4: You remember smells?

2: Yes, I remember.

5: You remember sights?

2: Yes. I remember.

5: You remember sights and smells together?

2: Yes. I remember. I remember nothing. Everything is happening now.

3: You remember tastes?

2: Yes. I remember.

1: You remember the feel of things?

2: Yes. I remember.

1: You remember the feel and the taste together?

2: Everything is happening now. Remembering is happening. Happening is constant.

5: Ah, Godfrey Burr, what an extraordinary length of time it is since we last met.

4: It is months since we last met. It is minutes since we last met. We never parted. To have known is to become.

5: Ah, Godfrey Burr, what an extraordinary length of time it is since we last met.

4: We last met in Disch, the capital of Plattah.

3: Years ago.

2: I remember.

1: I remember.

EMILY AND HEATHCLIFFE

1: Once again the lime trees are in blossom.

2: The next train to Putney leaves in twenty years.

1: Once again the turnips are in blossom.

2: My name is Heathcliffe.

1: My name is Emily Bronte.

2: My name is Heathcliffe.

1: It is a clear, fresh winter morning.

2: The next bus to Torquay leaves in twenty years.

1: Where will you be in twenty years, Heathcliffe?

2: My name is Pedro. My home is Catalonia. My heart is my heart.

1: Where will I be in twenty years, Heathcliffe?

2: You will be dead in twenty years. It is planned that you will die of tuberculosis.

1: Once again the plum trees are in blossom.

2: The next war begins in twenty years, Emily.

1: Where will you be in twenty years, Heathcliffe?

2: In Paris. I mean to live in Paris and have French-women.

1: Why?

2: It is the only way for a revolutionary that does not lead to hate.

1:    Once more the woods are green.

2:    There will be no more revolutions, Emily.

1:    The sky is ice, and beyond the sky there is ice. I know there is ice.

2:    You are wrong. There is fire.

1:    This vernal land once more wears feathers and petals. A dream is a static thing and there's the comfort.

2:    There will be no cottages for you, Emily. You will be dead in twenty years, dead as the train leaves for Putney, the bus for Torquay and the race for anger.

1:    I am dying of life, Heathcliffe.

I USED TO HAVE A FRIEND

1:    I used to have a friend.

2:    The Amazon is the greatest river in Sussex.

3:    The earth spins round the moon at a sickening rate.

2:    Fishing rights on the Amazon are reserved for debutantes.

4:    I used to have a friend too. He was a midget but he had the brain of a giant.

1:    My friend was a saint but he had the brain of a devil. He was also a Negro but he had the cunning of a debutante. He lived in Chile.

4:    I had another friend who was a cook but he had the soul of a marine engineer. He lived in Chile too.

3:    I had a friend who was Malayan but he had the nose of a Canadian. He lived in Canada but he made frequent visits to Chile.

2:    I had an aunt who lived in Chile but she had the vulgarity of a marine engineer.

4:    I had an aunt who was a marine engineer but she was as romantic as a fellow of the Royal Society.

5:    I had an aunt called Immanuel Kant.

3:    Jerusalem is the capital of Sussex.

4:    The best cricketers come from Jerusalem.

1:    Has anyone got any camembert?

2: I've got some obscene photographs. They show bishops blessing rockets.

3: The best rockets come from Jerusalem.

5: It's impossible to stand still.

4: I prefer the theatre to all other ways of stifling life.

3: The best theatres are in Jerusalem.

2: I prefer sexual intercourse to all other academic pursuits.

3: There is no sexual intercourse in Jerusalem.

1: I prefer sexual intercourse to the ultimate war between the nations.

5: In order for sexual intercourse to be successful it is essential to have sexes.

3: There are no sexes in Jerusalem.

2: Sexual intercourse was invented at the end of the last century by a man called Sigmund the Ripper.

3: Jerusalem is in decline. Thousands of years ago it was the centre of the contraceptive trade.

4: Contraceptive smuggling is increasing.

5: Contraceptive smugglers should be intercepted.

1: I love art.

4: I love art, too. I love art better than camembert.

3: I love art better than smuggling.

2: I once wrote a poem about some Greeks attacking a place called Troy. It had a modest success.

5: I once painted a picture of a woman with a silly smile. People seemed to like it.

1: I love art, but where does it get you?

3: It's a dodgy thing.

4: It's a chancy thing.

5: Bits of canvas.

2: Lamps of stone. Just hydrogen at bottom.

1: Like everything else.

3: And hydrogen goes bang.

4: Nineteen.

5: Eighteen.

2:   Seventeen.

3:   Sixteen.

5:   Fifteen.

3:   Fourteen.

1:   I had a friend - a long time ago.

METHUEN PLAYSCRIPTS

Michael Abbensetts	SWEET TALK
Paul Ableman	TESTS BLUE COMEDY
John Bowen	THE CORSICAN BROTHERS
Howard Brenton	REVENGE CHRISTIE IN LOVE and other plays PLAYS FOR PUBLIC PLACES MAGNIFICENCE
Peter Cheeseman (Ed)	THE KNOTTY
David Cregan	THREE MEN FOR COLVERTON TRANSCENDING and THE DANCERS THE HOUSES BY THE GREEN MINIATURES
Alan Cullen	THE STIRRINGS IN SHEFFIELD ON SATURDAY NIGHT
Simon Gray	THE IDIOT
Henry Livings	GOOD GRIEF! THE LITTLE MRS FOSTER SHOW HONOUR AND OFFER THIS JOCKEY DRIVES LATE NIGHTS THE FFINEST FFAMILY IN THE LAND EH? SIX MORE PONGO PLAYS INCLUDING TWO FO CHILDREN
John McGrath	EVENTS WHILE GUARDING THE BOFORS GUN
David Mercer	THE GOVERNOR'S LADY
Rodney Milgate	A REFINED LOOK AT EXISTENCE
Adrian Mitchell	MAN FRIDAY and MIND YOUR HEAD
Guillaume Oyono-Mbia	THREE SUITORS: ONE HUSBAND and UNTIL FURTHER NOTICE
Alan Plater	CLOSE THE COALHOUSE DOOR
Wole Soyinka	CAMWOOD ON THE LEAVES
Boris Vian	THE KNACKER'S ABC
Snoo Wilson	THE PLEASURE PRINCIPLE

NEW SHORT PLAYS

Carey Harrison	26 Efforts at Pornography
Leonard Melfi	Birdbath
Roger Howard	Four Plays for a Revolutionary Situation

NEW SHORT PLAYS: 2

Maureen Duffy	Rites
Carey Harrison	Lovers
Rochelle Owens	Futz

NEW SHORT PLAYS: 3

Howard Barker	Cheek
John Grillo	Number Three
Don Haworth	There's no Point in Arguing the Toss
Pip Simmons	Superman

If you would like regular information on new Methuen plays, please write to

The Marketing Department
Eyre Methuen Ltd
North Way
Andover
Hants